I Wonder Why
Greeks Built Temples

and other questions about Ancient Greece

Fiona Macdonald

KING*f*ISHER

KINGFISHER
Kingfisher Publications Plc,
New Penderel House,
283-288 High Holborn,
London, WC1V 7HZ
www.kingfisherpub.com

First published by Kingfisher Publications Plc 1997
First published in this format 2002
10 9 8 7 6 5 4 3

TS/1104/SHA/*UP UNV/126.6MA/F

A CIP catalogue record for this book is available from the
British Library

ISBN 0 7534 0756 6

Printed in Taiwan

Series editor: Clare Oliver
Series designer: David West Children's Books
Author: Fiona Macdonald
Consultant: Louise Schofield
Editor: Claire Llewellyn, Art editor: Christina Fraser
Picture researcher: Amanda Francis
Illustrations: Simone Boni (Virgil Pomfret) 26–27; Peter Dennis
(Linda Rogers) 8–9, 14–15, 24–25; Chris
Forsey cover; Terry Gabbey (AFA Ltd)
18–19; Luigi Galante (Virgil
Pomfret) 6–7, 16–17; Ian
Jackson 22–23, 30–31; Tony
Kenyon (BL Kearley) all cartoons;
Nicki Palin 20–21, 28–29;
Claudia Saraceni 12–13;
Thomas Trojer 10–11;
Richard Ward 4–5.

CONTENTS

4 Who were the Ancient Greeks?

5 Why did Greece grow bigger and bigger?

6 Was Greece one big happy country?

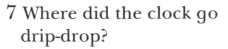

7 Where did the citizens take charge?

7 Where did the clock go drip-drop?

8 Who were the fiercest soldiers?

9 Who paid for weapons and armour?

10 Why did ships have long noses?

11 Why was it easier to travel by sea?

12 Who was goddess of wisdom?

13 Who told stories about the gods?

14 Who talked to the trees?

15 Where did Greeks empty their wine?

16 Why did Greeks build temples?

17 Whose fingers made their fortune?

18 When did a couple get married?

19 What did girls do all day?

19 Who went to the gym every day?

20 Why were Greek clothes so comfy?

21 Why were Greek shoes so bouncy?

21 Who took a shower in a bowl?

22 Where could you buy figs, beans, cheese and greens?

23 Why did farmers beat their trees?

23 Did the Greeks get drunk at breakfast?

24 Why did actors wear masks?

25 How did a tortoise make music?

26 Why were the Olympics held?

27 Did the winners get medals?

27 Who ran the first marathon?

28 Why did doctors ask so many questions?

28 Who had his best ideas in the bath?

29 Who discovered that the Earth is round?

30 How do we know about Ancient Greece?

31 Who copied the Greeks?

32 Index

Who were the Ancient Greeks?

The Ancient Greeks were people who lived in Greece from around 3,500 years ago. But they didn't live only in Greece. Some lived to the north and the east, in lands that we now call Bulgaria and Turkey. Others lived on small rocky islands in the Aegean Sea.

● Many Greek people set sail for North Africa, Turkey, Italy and France. They found safe harbours, where they built new homes and towns, and cleared the land for farming.

Greek homeland
Greek colonies

FRANCE
ITALY
Mediterranean Sea
NORTH AFRICA
Aegean Sea
TURKEY

● By 500BC the Greek world was large, rich and powerful. It stretched from France in the west to Turkey in the east.

● Wherever they went, the Greek settlers took their own way of life. They must have looked odd to the locals!

● The Greeks were a talented people. They had good laws and strong armies. They built beautiful temples and theatres. And they were great thinkers, artists and athletes.

Why did Greece grow bigger and bigger?

Greece and its homelands were small, and much of its land was too rocky for farming. By about 750BC, there was little room left for new towns or farms, and food began to run short. Because of this, many people left Greece to look for new places to live, and the Greek world began to grow.

Was Greece one big happy country?

Ancient Greece was not a single country like Greece is today. It was made up of different states, which were cut off from each other by high mountains, deep valleys, or the sea. The states weren't much bigger than cities, but they each had their own laws and army, and often quarrelled with each other. Athens was the biggest city-state.

● Each state was made up of a city and the surrounding countryside. Many city-states lay close to the sea, and had a harbour, too.

HARBOUR

TEMPLE

PRISON

AGORA

SCHOOL

CITY WALLS

FARMLAND

● Sparta was a city-state in southern Greece. It was ruled by two kings from two royal families, who were helped by a council of wise old men.

THEATRE

HOUSES

● Most wealthy Greek households had slaves. The slaves did all the hard work, such as building, farming, housework and looking after the children.

Where did the citizens take charge?

In Athens, all grown men who weren't slaves were citizens. They could choose their government officials and vote for or against new laws. Citizens could also speak at the Assembly. This was a huge open-air meeting where people stood up and told the government what it should be doing.

● There had to be at least 6,000 citizens at every Assembly. They all met on the slopes of a hill in Athens, and voted by raising their hand.

Where did the clock go drip-drop?

Citizens who spoke at the Assembly weren't allowed to drone on for too long. Each speaker was timed with a water clock. When the last drop of water had dripped out of the jar, his time was up. He had to sit down and hold his tongue!

Who were the fiercest soldiers?

The soldiers of Sparta were the fiercest army in Ancient Greece. They were brave, ruthless and very well-trained. None of the men had ordinary jobs, even in peacetime. They spent their whole lives just training and fighting.

● Spartan warriors were famous for their long flowing hair. Before a battle, they sat down and combed it. Perhaps their long manes made them feel like lions!

● For Spartans, bravery was more important than anything else. To punish cowards, they shaved off half their hair and half their beard! This was a terrible disgrace.

Who paid for weapons and armour?

● Greek soldiers fought side by side in tight rows called phalanxes. Each soldier's shield overlapped his neighbour's, making a strong wall of shields that protected all of them.

Greek soldiers had to buy their own weapons and armour. A wealthy soldier bought himself a sharp spear and sword, a strong shield, and expensive body armour. But a poor soldier made do with whatever he could find. And sometimes this was little more than an animal skin and a wooden club!

● In Sparta it wasn't just the men who had to be fit. Women had to do lots of exercises to make sure their babies were healthy and strong.

● After winning a battle, soldiers sometimes gave their armour to the gods as a thank-you present. They laid it inside a temple or hung it on the branches of a tree.

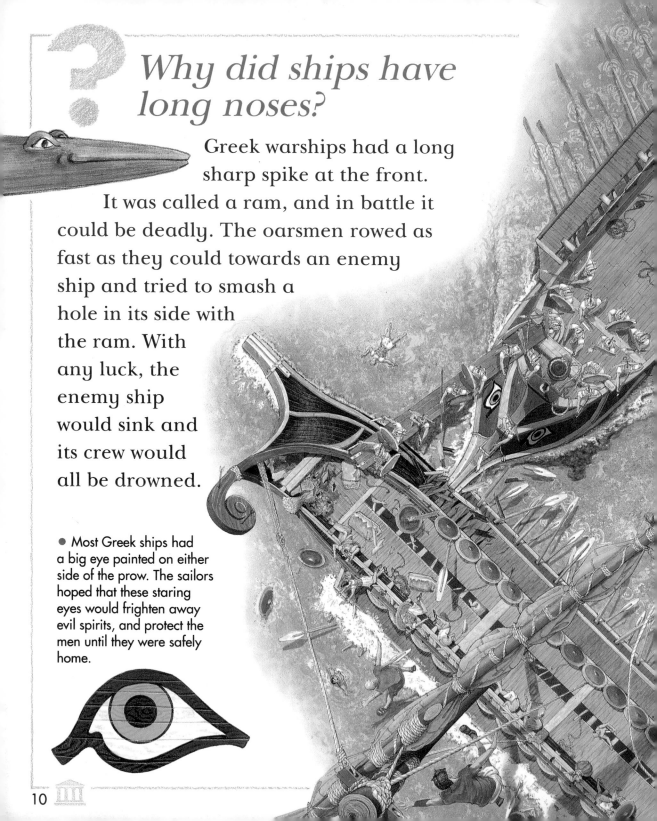

Why did ships have long noses?

Greek warships had a long sharp spike at the front. It was called a ram, and in battle it could be deadly. The oarsmen rowed as fast as they could towards an enemy ship and tried to smash a hole in its side with the ram. With any luck, the enemy ship would sink and its crew would all be drowned.

● Most Greek ships had a big eye painted on either side of the prow. The sailors hoped that these staring eyes would frighten away evil spirits, and protect the men until they were safely home.

- The biggest warships were called triremes, and had three rows of oarsmen along each side of the boat. With 170 men pulling on the oars, ships zipped through the water at an amazing speed.

- Each ship had a flute-player who piped tunes with a steady beat. The oarsmen all pulled their oars in time with the music, which meant they didn't get all tangled up!

Why was it easier to travel by sea?

There are many islands in Greece and boats are often still the only way to get from one island to another. But the Ancient Greeks used boats to get around the mainland too. Sailing along the coast was much quicker and easier than struggling up steep, stony tracks on the back of a weary donkey!

Who was goddess of wisdom?

Athene was the goddess of war and also of wisdom, and so her symbol was the wise owl. She had special powers to protect the city of Athens. Because of this, the citizens loved and worshipped her. They built Athene her very own temple, the Parthenon, high on the Acropolis, a hill overlooking the city.

• According to stories, the gods lived on top of Mount Olympus, the highest mountain in Greece. But they didn't always behave as you'd expect gods to – they spent a lot of their time quarrelling!

Hermes messenger of the gods

Zeus king of the gods

Demeter goddess of crops

Aphrodite goddess of love and beauty

Hera queen of the gods, goddess of women and children

Hades god of the underworld

● The Greeks believed in many different gods and goddesses. Each one had different powers. Some of the gods were kind, but others were stern and cruel.

Who told stories about the gods?

A famous poet called Homer told many exciting stories about gods and heroes. His long poem *The Odyssey* tells the adventures of Odysseus, a Greek soldier sailing home to Ithaca from the war with Troy. The sea god Poseidon tries to sink his ship, but with Athene's protection, Odysseus finally gets home.

● Poseidon was god of the sea. He tried to sink Odysseus's ship by stirring up violent storms.

● Inside the Parthenon stood a towering statue of Athene – about ten times taller than you! It was covered with precious gold and ivory.

Who talked to the trees?

The Greeks believed that nature goddesses called dryads lived deep in the woods. Priests and priestesses guarded the holy woods and prayed to the dryads. Then they listened hard for any rustlings in the trees – which might be the nature goddesses' messages in reply!

● According to legend, dryads wore crowns of leaves and danced in the woods. They also carried axes – to attack anyone who damaged their trees.

- There were over 40 religious holidays in Athens each year. There are paintings of these festivals on wine jars and other Greek pottery. People loved festivals. They didn't have to work and there was lots of free food and drink.

- Wealthy people took animals to the temple to be sacrificed to the gods. But poor people couldn't afford to give their own animals – so they took pastry ones instead.

Where did Greeks empty their wine?

Many Greeks prayed to the gods in their own homes at a special altar. They liked to offer the gods presents of food or wine. Sometimes, worshippers poured a whole jar of wine over the altar. More often, they drank most of the wine themselves, and just gave the gods a tiny drop!

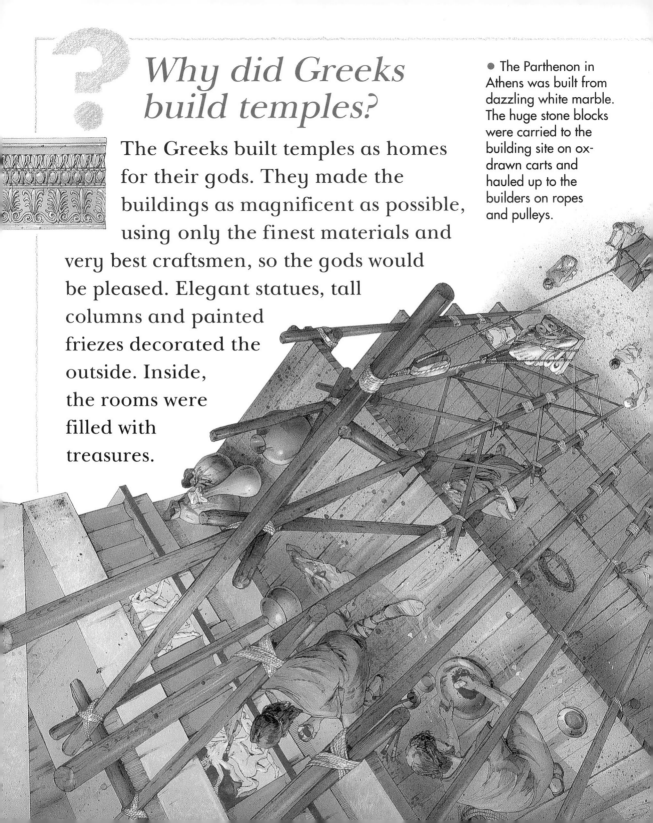

Why did Greeks build temples?

The Greeks built temples as homes for their gods. They made the buildings as magnificent as possible, using only the finest materials and very best craftsmen, so the gods would be pleased. Elegant statues, tall columns and painted friezes decorated the outside. Inside, the rooms were filled with treasures.

● The Parthenon in Athens was built from dazzling white marble. The huge stone blocks were carried to the building site on ox-drawn carts and hauled up to the builders on ropes and pulleys.

Whose fingers made their fortune?

Greek craftsmen were very skilful, and made beautiful works of art. Stonemasons carved marble figures, metalworkers made statues and vases of bronze, while potters and painters made wonderful jars and flasks. Some craftsmen became rich and famous and sold their work abroad as well as at home.

● Greek potters were famous for their beautiful bowls, vases and cups. They worked with artists, who decorated the pottery in red or black, with paintings of heroes, gods or ordinary people.

● Greek sculptors carved wonderful statues. One story tells how the sculptor Pygmalion made such a lifelike statue of a woman that he fell in love with it! Aphrodite, the goddess of love, took pity on him and brought the statue to life.

● Temple columns weren't made from one single piece of stone. They were built from drum-shaped pieces held together by pegs. The pieces fitted together snugly – so long as you put them in the right order!

When did a couple get married?

Most couples got married when their parents said so! A wealthy father wanted a good match for his son or daughter – one that would make the family even richer and more important. Greek brides were only 13 or 14 years old when they got married. Their husbands were usually much older – 30, at least.

● On her wedding day, the bride was driven in a chariot to her new husband's home. There was laughter and music, and burning torches to light the way.

● The bride's chariot was broken after the wedding, as a sign that she could never go back to her old home.

What did girls do all day?

Young girls from wealthy families were sometimes taught to read at home, but girls didn't go to school. Most learnt from their mother how to spin fleece into thread, and then weave it into fine woollen cloth. Greek women made all the cloth their families needed – for wall hangings, blankets and rugs as well as for clothes.

● A Greek legend tells the story of a girl called Arachne, who thought she was better at spinning than the goddess Athene. Athene was so angry that she turned Arachne into a spider. Then all she could spin was a web!

● A few women did learn to read and write. One of the most famous Greek poets was a woman called Sappho, who lived about 2,500 years ago.

Who went to the gym every day?

'Gym' is short for 'gymnasium', the Greek name for school. Boys went to school from about the age of seven. They learnt all the usual things like reading, writing and maths, as well as how to make a speech, recite poetry and sing.

Why were Greek clothes so comfy?

The Greeks wore light, loose-fitting clothes. There were no tight buttons or zips, just flowing robes or simple tunics called chitons (say *kit-owns*). Chitons were just big squares of cloth, draped over the body and held in place by pins at the shoulders and a belt round the waist.

● The Greeks liked brightly-coloured clothes, decorated with embroidery. Most clothes were made out of wool or linen, but rich people wore silk, too.

● Greek women liked to wear lots of jewellery. Wealthy ones wore gold and silver bracelets, necklaces and dangly earrings that jingled with every move.

Why were Greek shoes so bouncy?

Most Greeks liked to go barefoot in the house. But when they went out, they wore cool summer sandals or warm winter boots. The comfiest ones had thick soles made of cork. This made them soft and bouncy – just right for walking on stony ground.

● The Greeks wore wide-brimmed hats made of plaited straw to protect themselves from the scorching summer sun.

Who took a shower in a bowl?

When the Ancient Greeks wanted a shower, they stripped off and crouched inside a deep pottery bowl. Then a slave would come and pour jars of cool, refreshing water all over them.

Where could you buy figs, beans, cheese and greens?

Town-dwellers bought their food at the agora, the open-air market in the centre of town. There was always plenty of fresh fruit, vegetables and grain – all grown on farms just outside town. You could also buy cheeses made from goat's or sheep's milk, which were flavoured with sweet-smelling herbs.

● Every year after the grape harvest, people had to jump into big wooden tubs, and crush the fruit into juice to make wine. It was hot, tiring and sticky work.

● Farmers loaded their donkeys with food to sell at the agora – fruit and vegetables, cheeses, chickens and a squealing piglet or two!

Why did farmers beat their trees?

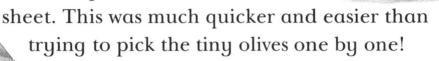

Before farmers harvested their olives, they spread huge sheets of cloth under the trees. Then they whacked the branches to make all the ripe fruit fall on the sheet. This was much quicker and easier than trying to pick the tiny olives one by one!

● Ordinary people rarely bought meat because it was much too expensive. So when they did, they ate every scrap. They fried the lungs, stewed the intestines and boiled the brains!

Did the Greeks get drunk at breakfast?

Certainly not! Some Greeks did drink wine at breakfast, but it was mixed with plenty of water. Most people preferred milk. Favourite breakfast foods included bread, porridge, eggs, fish, or a few figs.

Why did actors wear masks?

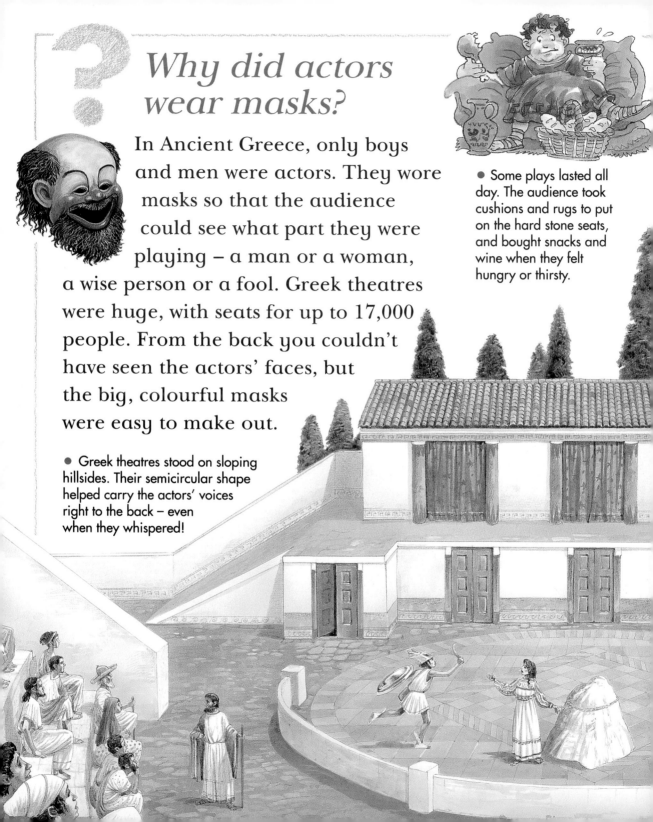

In Ancient Greece, only boys and men were actors. They wore masks so that the audience could see what part they were playing – a man or a woman, a wise person or a fool. Greek theatres were huge, with seats for up to 17,000 people. From the back you couldn't have seen the actors' faces, but the big, colourful masks were easy to make out.

● Some plays lasted all day. The audience took cushions and rugs to put on the hard stone seats, and bought snacks and wine when they felt hungry or thirsty.

● Greek theatres stood on sloping hillsides. Their semicircular shape helped carry the actors' voices right to the back – even when they whispered!

How did a tortoise make music?

Sad to say, a tortoise only made music when it was dead. An empty tortoiseshell was used to make a lyre, a musical instrument rather like a harp. Musicians fixed strings to the shell and plucked them to play a tune.

• The double flute was another popular musical instrument but it was difficult to play. You needed twice as much puff as for a single flute, and each hand played a different tune.

• Theatre staff carried big sticks in case of trouble. Sometimes the huge audience got carried away by a play and began to riot. A few hefty whacks soon quietened them down!

Why were the Olympics held?

The Olympic Games were part of a religious festival in honour of Zeus, king of the gods. Every four years, 20,000 people flocked to Olympia to watch athletes run, box, wrestle, and race chariots. The hardest event of all was the pentathlon. Contestants had to take part in five different sports – the long jump, running, wrestling, throwing the discus and throwing the javelin.

● Women were banned from the Olympics. They held their own games, in honour of Hera, queen of the gods. The women's games had only one event, which was running.

● At the Olympics all the athletes were naked. The Greeks were proud of their bodies, and weren't afraid to show them off!

Did the winners get medals?

Winning at the Olympics was a great honour, just as it is today. But there were no medals in the ancient games. Instead, the winners got crowns made of laurel leaves, jars of olive oil, beautiful pots or vases, and pieces of wool, silk or linen to make into clothes.

● Greek boxers didn't wear padded gloves like boxers today. They simply wrapped strips of leather around their fists.

Who ran the first marathon?

In 490BC the Greeks won a battle at Marathon, about 42 kilometres from Athens. A Greek soldier called Pheidippides ran all the way to Athens to tell the citizens the good news. Sadly, his 'marathon' exhausted him, and the poor man collapsed and died.

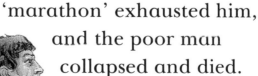

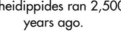

● There was no marathon race in the ancient games, but there is today. It measures 42 kilometres – exactly the same distance that poor Pheidippides ran 2,500 years ago.

Why did doctors ask so many questions?

Greek doctors knew it was important to find out as much as they could about their patients. So they asked them all sorts of questions – what sort of food they ate, whether they took any exercise, and so on. People had once believed illness was a punishment from the gods, but Greek doctors had more scientific ideas.

Who had his best ideas in the bath?

Archimedes was a mathematician who lived in Greece around 250BC. One day when he was in the bath, he finally worked out a problem that had been troubling him for ages. He was so excited he jumped out of the bath shouting 'Eureka!' ('I've got it!'), and ran down the street to tell his friends!

• The Greeks loved learning about new ideas. They would sit under a shady tree and talk for hours about all sorts of things, from the way people lived to the future of the world.

Who discovered that the Earth is round?

Greek scientists were very interested in the Earth and space. In about 470BC, a scientist called Parmenides was watching an eclipse of the Moon. He noticed the Earth cast a dark, curved shadow on the Moon, and worked out that if the shadow was curved then the Earth must be round!

• One famous Greek thinker was called Diogenes. He lived in an old wooden barrel so people could see that he didn't care about money or possessions. He was only interested in ideas.

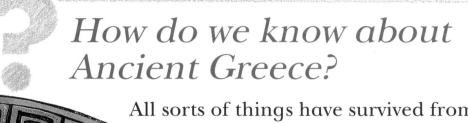

How do we know about Ancient Greece?

All sorts of things have survived from Ancient Greece – not just buildings and statues, but also writings, weapons, jewellery and coins. Historians study these things carefully. They look for clues to piece together a picture of the past, just as detectives look for clues in a case.

● Greek pottery tells us a lot about life in Ancient Greece. It's decorated with pictures of families at home, athletes, festivals and people at work. Can you guess what job the man on this plate did?